Table Of Contents

Chapter 1: Introduction to Healthy Cooking for Parents and Children — 4

- The Importance of Cooking Together as a Family — 5
- Benefits of Teaching Kids to Cook — 6
- Creating a Kid-Friendly Kitchen Environment — 7
- Meal Planning for Busy Families — 8
- Stocking a Healthy Pantry — 11
- Essential Kitchen Tools for Cooking with Kids — 12

Chapter 3: Breakfast Delights — 15

- Energizing Smoothies and Smoothie Bowls — 16
- Creative Pancake Variations — 17
- Wholesome Oatmeal Creations — 19

Chapter 4: Lunchbox Favorites — 22

- Packing Nutritious and Delicious School Lunches — 23
- Easy-to-Make Wraps and Roll-ups — 23

Fun and Healthy Snack Ideas	26
Chapter 5: Kid-Friendly Dinners	**28**
Homemade Pizza Night	29
Build-Your-Own Tacos and Burritos	31
One-Pot Wonder Meals	31
Chapter 6: Sweet Treats and Snacks	**35**
Healthy Baking with Kids	36
Delectable Fruit-Based Desserts	37
Guilt-Free Snack Options	40
Chapter 7: Exploring International Cuisines	**42**
Introduction to Different Cultures' Foods	43
Cooking Easy and Tasty Ethnic Dishes	44
Creating a Global Food Experience at Home	46
Chapter 8: Fun Cooking Activities and Projects	**49**
Edible Crafts for Kids	50
Growing Your Own Kitchen Garden	50
Hosting a Kids' Cooking Party	53
Chapter 9: Tips for Picky Eaters	**56**
Dealing with Selective Eating Habits	57
Sneaking in Hidden Veggies	59
Making Mealtime Fun and Stress-Free	60

Chapter 10: Nurturing a Lifelong Love for Healthy Cooking — 64

- Encouraging Culinary Curiosity in Children — 65
- Teaching Kitchen Safety and Basic Cooking Skills — 67
- Making Cooking a Family Tradition — 69

Chapter 11: Conclusion — 72

- Reflecting on the Journey of Cooking with Kids — 73
- Final Thoughts and Encouragement for Parents and Children — 75

Appendix: — 78

- Kid-Friendly Kitchen Tools and Equipment Checklist — 79
- Sample Weekly Meal Plan — 80
- Nutritional Guidelines for Children — 83
- Glossary of Cooking Terms — 84

Chapter 1: Introduction to Healthy Cooking for Parents and Children

The Importance of Cooking Together as a Family

In today's fast-paced world, finding quality time to spend with our loved ones can be a challenge. However, one activity that can bring families closer together is cooking. Cooking together not only creates lasting memories but also provides numerous benefits for both parents and children. In this subchapter, we will explore the importance of cooking together as a family.

One of the key advantages of cooking as a family is the promotion of healthy meal prep. Involving children in the kitchen allows them to develop a positive relationship with food and learn about the importance of balanced nutrition. By engaging children in meal planning and preparation, parents can teach them about the various food groups, portion control, and the benefits of cooking with fresh ingredients. This hands-on experience encourages children to make healthier food choices and instills a sense of responsibility for their own well-being.

Cooking together also fosters creativity and a sense of accomplishment for children. By allowing them to participate in meal preparation, parents can empower their children to express themselves through food. Whether it's mixing ingredients, chopping vegetables, or decorating a cake, children can unleash their imagination and develop their culinary skills. This not only boosts their self-confidence but also cultivates a lifelong passion for cooking and healthy eating.

Moreover, cooking as a family strengthens the bond between parents and children. It provides an opportunity for open communication, laughter, and shared experiences. As parents and children work side by side in the kitchen, they learn to collaborate, problem-solve, and appreciate each other's contributions. Cooking together becomes a time to connect, relax, and enjoy each other's company, away from the distractions of technology and daily routines.

In the book "Kid-Friendly Kitchen: Fun and Healthy Recipes for Parents and Children," we offer a variety of delicious and nutritious recipes that are easy to prepare and enjoyable for the whole family. Each recipe is specially designed to engage children in the cooking process, making it a fun and educational experience for both parents and little ones.

In conclusion, cooking together as a family has numerous benefits for parents and children. From promoting healthy meal prep to fostering creativity and strengthening family bonds, the kitchen becomes a hub of learning, love, and laughter. So, grab your aprons, gather your loved ones, and let's embark on a journey of culinary exploration and togetherness.

Benefits of Teaching Kids to Cook

Promotes Healthy Eating Habits:

By involving kids in meal preparation, parents can instill healthy eating habits from an early age. Children who cook their meals are more likely to make nutritious choices and develop a taste for healthy foods. They become aware of the ingredients used in their favorite dishes, encouraging them to make conscious decisions about what they eat.

Enhances Essential Life Skills:

Cooking is a valuable life skill that teaches children about planning, organization, and time management. Measuring ingredients, following recipes, and understanding cooking techniques improve their math and reading skills. Additionally, cooking encourages creativity and problem-solving, as children learn to substitute ingredients and adapt recipes to their liking.

Boosts Confidence and Independence:

As children gain confidence in the kitchen, they become more independent and self-reliant. Learning to cook empowers them to take charge of their own meals, reducing reliance on processed or unhealthy foods. Preparing a dish from start to finish and receiving praise for their efforts boosts their self-esteem and encourages a positive relationship with food.

Fosters Family Bonding:

Cooking together provides an opportunity for parents and children to connect and bond. It becomes a shared experience, where families can create lasting memories and traditions. Through teamwork in the kitchen, children learn cooperation, communication, and respect for others' contributions.

Cultivates Cultural Appreciation:

Introducing kids to different cuisines through cooking exposes them to diverse cultures and promotes appreciation for global flavors. Exploring international recipes helps broaden their culinary horizons and encourages them to be open to new tastes, textures, and ingredients.

Creating a Kid-Friendly Kitchen Environment

In today's fast-paced world, where convenience often trumps nutrition, it is increasingly important for parents to be proactive in promoting healthy eating habits for their children. One of the most effective ways to achieve this is by creating a kid-friendly kitchen environment. This subchapter will provide practical tips and ideas to help parents and children transform their kitchen into a space that promotes fun and healthy cooking and meal preparation.

First and foremost, it is crucial to design a kitchen layout that is safe and accessible for children:

Ensure that cooking utensils, pots, and pans are stored within reach, so kids can actively participate in meal prep without straining or risking accidents. Consider investing in child-sized cookware and utensils, allowing them to feel more involved and confident in the kitchen. Organizing the pantry and refrigerator Arrange healthy snacks, such as cut fruits and vegetables, in easily accessible containers at eye level.

Label shelves or use colorful baskets to clearly designate specific food groups, making it easier for kids to choose a balanced meal.

Furthermore, engaging children in the meal planning process can greatly increase their interest in eating healthily. Design a weekly menu together, ensuring it includes a variety of fruits, vegetables, whole grains, and lean proteins. Consider incorporating themed nights or allowing children to choose a recipe they would like to try. By involving them in the decision-making process, children will develop a sense of ownership and excitement about their meals.

To foster a positive cooking experience, create a designated space for children to experiment and explore their culinary creativity. Set up a kid-friendly cooking station with age-appropriate tools and ingredients. Encourage them to experiment with new flavors and textures, fostering a sense of adventure and curiosity in the kitchen. Lastly, make cooking a family affair. Cooking together not only strengthens bonds but also encourages children to learn from their parents' positive cooking habits. Take turns sharing kitchen responsibilities, such as chopping vegetables or stirring a sauce. This will instill a sense of teamwork and create lasting memories.

Chapter 2: Basics of Healthy Meal Prep

Meal Planning for Busy Families

It can be a challenge for busy families to find the time to prepare healthy meals between work, school, extracurricular activities, and other commitments, it's easy to resort to fast food or takeout. However, with a little bit of planning and organization, you can ensure that your family enjoys delicious and nutritious meals every day.

Meal planning is a crucial tool for busy families. It not only saves time but also helps you make healthier choices. By planning your meals in advance, you can avoid the last-minute scramble to figure out what to cook and end up making unhealthy choices. Here are some tips to help you get started on your meal planning journey:

1. Set aside a specific time each week to plan your meals. This could be a weekend morning or even a quiet evening during the week. Get your children involved in the process by asking for their input on what they would like to eat.

2. Create a weekly meal calendar. Start by listing the days of the week and then fill in the meals for each day. Consider including a variety of proteins, vegetables, and grains to ensure a balanced diet.

3. Make a shopping list based on your meal plan. Take inventory of your pantry and refrigerator before heading to the grocery store. This will help you avoid buying unnecessary items and reduce food waste.

4. Prepare ingredients in advance. Spend some time chopping vegetables, marinating meats, or pre-cooking grains over the weekend. This will save you time during the busy weekdays and make cooking a breeze.

5. Get creative with leftovers. Plan meals that can be repurposed into delicious new dishes. For example, leftover roasted chicken can be turned into a flavorful chicken salad or added to a stir-fry.

6. Involve your children in meal preparation. Kids are more likely to eat healthy meals if they have a hand in preparing them. Give them age-appropriate tasks like washing vegetables, stirring ingredients, or setting the table.

Remember, meal planning is not about perfection; it's about creating a system that works for your family. Be flexible and willing to adapt as needed. By incorporating these meal planning strategies into your routine, you'll be well on your way to providing delicious and healthy meals for your busy family.

Stocking a Healthy Pantry

In order to maintain a healthy and balanced diet, it is essential to have a well-stocked pantry. Having nutritious ingredients readily available not only makes cooking easier, but also encourages children to make healthier food choices. In this subchapter, we will explore the key items to stock in your pantry to ensure you can prepare delicious and nutritious meals for your family.

1. Whole Grains: Whole grains are an excellent source of fiber, vitamins, and minerals. Stock your pantry with whole wheat pasta, brown rice, quinoa, and whole grain bread. These options are not only healthier but also more filling, keeping your children satisfied for longer periods of time.

2. Canned Goods: Canned goods can be a lifesaver when it comes to quick and healthy meals. Opt for low-sodium canned beans, diced tomatoes, and canned tuna or salmon packed in water. These versatile ingredients can be used in a variety of dishes, from hearty soups to tasty salads.

3. Healthy Oils: Choose heart-healthy oils like olive oil or avocado oil for cooking and dressings. These oils provide essential fatty acids and can add a delicious flavor to your dishes.

4. Nut and Seed Butters: Nut and seed butters, such as almond butter or sunflower seed butter, are great sources of protein and healthy fats. They can be spread on whole grain bread, added to smoothies, or used as a dip for fruits and vegetables.

5. Spices and Herbs: Stock your pantry with a variety of spices and herbs to enhance the flavor of your meals without adding excess salt or sugar. Experiment with different combinations to create delicious and kid-friendly flavors.

6. Snacks: Having healthy snacks on hand is essential for busy families. Stock your pantry with dried fruits, unsalted nuts, whole grain crackers, and popcorn. These snacks are not only tasty but also provide important nutrients to support your child's growth and development.

Remember, a well-stocked pantry sets the foundation for healthy eating habits. By having these essential items readily available, you can easily prepare nutritious meals that your children will love. Get creative in the kitchen, involve your children in meal prep, and enjoy the benefits of a healthy and flavorful diet together as a family.

Essential Kitchen Tools for Cooking with Kids

To make the most of your cooking adventures, it is essential to have the right kitchen tools on hand. Here are some must-have kitchen tools for cooking with kids.

1. Child-sized Aprons and Oven Mitts

These adorable aprons protect your little ones' clothing from spills and stains, while oven mitts keep their hands safe when handling hot pots and pans.

2. Safety Knives

Introducing kids to knives can be a bit daunting, but safety knives are specifically designed to make this task easier. These knives have blunt edges, reducing the risk of accidents, while still allowing children to practice cutting skills under adult supervision.

3. Mixing Bowls and Measuring Cups

Mixing bowls and measuring cups are indispensable tools in the kitchen. They allow kids to measure and mix ingredients accurately and provide an opportunity to teach them about portion control and following recipes.

4. Silicone Baking Mats
Silicone baking mats are a fantastic addition to any kitchen, especially when cooking with kids. These mats prevent food from sticking to the baking sheet and make clean-up a breeze. They are also reusable and environmentally friendly.

5. Vegetable Peelers
Vegetable peelers are excellent tools for teaching kids about different types of products and how to prepare them. Look for peelers with an ergonomic handle and a blade cover for added safety.

6. Miniature Utensils
Small, child-sized utensils are perfect for little hands. Invest in mini spatulas, whisks, and tongs to allow kids to participate fully in the cooking process. These tools are not only safer for children but also make cooking more enjoyable for them.

7. Slow Cooker
A slow cooker can be a lifesaver for busy parents. It allows for easy and convenient meal preparation, making it an excellent tool when cooking with kids. Kids can help assemble the ingredients, and the slow cooker does the rest of the work, resulting in a delicious and healthy meal.

By having these essential kitchen tools, parents and children can create a safe and enjoyable cooking environment. Cooking together fosters bonding, promotes healthy meal prep, and instills a love for cooking and nutritious eating habits in children. So, gather your little chefs, put on those aprons, and embark on a culinary adventure that will create lasting memories for the whole family.

Chapter 3: Breakfast Delights

Energizing Smoothies and Smoothie Bowls

It can be challenging for parents to ensure that their children are getting all the essential nutrients they need. However, with the rising popularity of smoothies and smoothie bowls, it has become easier than ever to create delicious and nutritious meals that both parents and children can enjoy.

Smoothies are versatile and can be tailored to suit individual tastes and dietary needs. They are an excellent way to incorporate fruits, vegetables, and other nutrient-rich ingredients into your child's diet. Not only are they packed with vitamins and minerals, but they also provide a great source of energy to kick-start your child's day or to refuel after an active afternoon.

We have compiled a collection of energizing smoothie and smoothie bowl recipes that will appeal to both parents and children. These recipes are not only delicious but also easy to prepare, making them perfect for busy families. So, grab a blender and join us in the kitchen for some delicious and nutritious smoothie adventures!

One of our favorite recipes is the **"Berry Blast Smoothie Bowl."** This colorful and refreshing bowl is loaded with antioxidants from mixed berries, providing a boost to your child's immune system. Topped with crunchy granola and sliced bananas, it is a feast for the senses and a great way to start the day. For those seeking a protein-packed option, our **"Peanut Butter Banana Smoothie"** is a hit. This creamy and indulgent smoothie is made with peanut butter, banana, and Greek yogurt, providing a healthy dose of protein and essential nutrients. It's perfect for a quick snack or a post-workout treat.

We also understand the importance of variety, which is why we have included recipes that cater to different dietary preferences. Our **"Green Goddess Smoothie"** is an excellent option for those wanting to incorporate more greens into their child's diet. Packed with spinach, avocado, and pineapple, it is not only nutritious but also deliciously refreshing.

With these energizing smoothie and smoothie bowl recipes, parents can rest assured that their children are getting the nutrition they need in a fun and enjoyable way. By involving children in the preparation process, parents can also encourage healthy eating habits and cultivate an appreciation for cooking from an early age.

Creative Pancake Variations

Pancakes are a beloved breakfast staple for both kids and adults alike. They are not only delicious but also incredibly versatile. In this subchapter, we will explore some creative pancake variations that will make mealtime a fun and exciting experience for parents and children. So, grab your spatula and get ready to flip some pancakes that will bring smiles to the faces of both parents and children alike!

1. Fruity Delights: Add a burst of freshness and natural sweetness to your pancakes by incorporating various fruits. Mash up some ripe bananas and mix them into your pancake batter for a tropical twist. Alternatively, try adding blueberries, strawberries, or even grated apples for a burst of flavor and added nutrients.

2. Chocolate Lovers' Dream: Who doesn't love a touch of chocolate? For all the chocolate enthusiasts out there, you can easily transform your regular pancakes into a chocolatey delight. Simply add a tablespoon or two of cocoa powder to your batter and mix well. Top it off with a drizzle of melted chocolate or a sprinkle of chocolate chips for an extra indulgent treat.

3. Savory Pancakes: Pancakes don't always have to be sweet. Experiment with savory variations to create a nutritious and filling meal. Add shredded cheese, diced vegetables, or even cooked bacon to your batter before cooking. These savory pancakes are perfect for lunch or dinner and can be served with a side salad or a dollop of sour cream.

4. Pancake Stacks: Take your pancake game to another level by creating pancake stacks. Layer your pancakes with a variety of fillings such as Nutella, peanut butter, or fruit compote. Stack them up high and let your little ones have fun with assembling their own pancake tower. This interactive meal is not only visually appealing but also encourages creativity and fine motor skills.

5. Pancake Pops: Make breakfast more exciting by turning your pancakes into popsicles. Simply prepare mini pancakes using cookie cutters or molds. Insert a popsicle stick into each pancake and serve them with a variety of dipping sauces such as maple syrup, yogurt, or fruit puree. These pancake pops are not only adorable but also make breakfast on-the-go a breeze.

These creative pancake variations are not only delicious but also offer a great opportunity to introduce new flavors and ingredients to picky eaters. By involving your children in the cooking process, you can encourage them to explore new tastes and become more adventurous eaters.

Wholesome Oatmeal Creations

Oatmeal is not only delicious, but it is also a nutritious breakfast option for both parents and children. Packed with fiber, vitamins, and minerals, this versatile grain provides a great start to your day. In this subchapter, we will explore some creative and kid-friendly recipes that will make oatmeal an exciting part of your morning routine.

1. Berry Blast Overnight Oats: Overnight oats are a fantastic option for busy parents. Simply mix rolled oats, milk (or a dairy-free alternative), a dollop of honey, and a handful of mixed berries in a jar. Leave it in the fridge overnight, and wake up to a delightful breakfast that is ready to be enjoyed!

2. Banana Split Oatmeal: Who said oatmeal can't be fun? This recipe takes inspiration from the classic ice cream dessert. Cook your oats as usual and top them with sliced bananas, a drizzle of honey, a sprinkle of granola, and a dollop of Greek yogurt. It's a balanced and delicious breakfast that will make your little ones smile.

3. Apple Cinnamon Baked Oatmeal: Baked oatmeal is a fantastic meal prep option for busy mornings. Mix together oats, diced apples, cinnamon, milk, eggs, and a touch of maple syrup. Pour the mixture into a baking dish and bake until golden and set. Cut into squares and refrigerate for a grab-and-go breakfast option throughout the week.

4. Oatmeal Pancakes: Pancakes can still be healthy! Blend rolled oats, milk, eggs, a ripe banana, and a dash of cinnamon in a blender until smooth. Pour the batter onto a hot griddle and cook until golden brown. Serve with fresh fruit and a drizzle of honey for a wholesome twist on a breakfast classic.

5. Oatmeal Energy Balls: Looking for a convenient and nutritious snack for your little ones? Combine oats, nut butter, honey, and a handful of chocolate chips in a bowl. Roll the mixture into bite-sized balls and refrigerate. These energy balls are perfect for an on-the-go snack or a quick pick-me-up during the day.

These wholesome oatmeal creations are just the beginning of the endless possibilities that oatmeal offers. Get creative and involve your children in the kitchen! By encouraging them to experiment with different flavors and toppings, you can instill a love for healthy cooking and create lasting memories together.

Chapter 4: Lunchbox Favorites

Packing Nutritious and Delicious School Lunches

When it comes to healthy meal prep, it is essential to include a variety of food groups in your child's lunchbox. Aim for a balanced meal that includes whole grains, lean proteins, fruits, vegetables, and dairy or dairy alternatives. This ensures that your child gets the necessary nutrients to fuel their day and support their growth and development.

To make the process more engaging for children, involve them in meal planning and preparation. Encourage them to choose their favorite fruits and vegetables, and let them help with washing and cutting. This way, they will be more likely to enjoy their lunches and develop healthy eating habits.

One idea for a delicious and nutritious school lunch is a **colorful and appealing salad**. Create a salad bar at home with a variety of vegetables, such as cherry tomatoes, cucumbers, carrots, and bell peppers. Let your child choose their favorite toppings, such as grilled chicken, boiled eggs, or chickpeas. Pack a separate container of homemade dressing for them to drizzle over their salad at lunchtime.

Another creative option is to make **wraps or pinwheels using whole wheat tortillas**. Fill them with lean deli meats, cheese, and a selection of veggies. Roll them tightly and slice into bite-sized pieces. These bite-sized wraps are not only visually appealing but also easy for little hands to hold and eat.

For a **sweet treat,** consider packing fresh fruit skewers or homemade energy balls. These provide a natural source of sweetness and energy without the added sugars found in many store-bought snacks.

Remember, the key to successful school lunches is variety and balance. Try to avoid repetitive meals and include a mix of flavors, textures, and colors to keep your child excited about their lunches. With a little creativity and planning, packing nutritious and delicious school lunches can become a fun and enjoyable activity for both parents and children.

Easy-to-Make Wraps and Roll-ups

Wraps and roll-ups are not only delicious, but they also provide a great opportunity to get creative in the kitchen. They are perfect for busy parents who want to prepare healthy meals for their children in a fun and convenient way.

1. **Veggie Delight Wrap:** This wrap is loaded with colorful vegetables that are not only tasty but also packed with essential nutrients. Start with a whole wheat tortilla and spread a layer of hummus or cream cheese. Then, add a variety of veggies such as sliced cucumbers, bell peppers, shredded carrots, and baby spinach leaves. Roll it up and secure it with toothpicks. This wrap is perfect for kids who are hesitant to eat their veggies.

2. **Turkey Club Roll-up:** Kids love the classic flavors of a club sandwich, and this roll-up version is a healthier alternative. Lay a large lettuce leaf on a tortilla and layer it with sliced turkey, turkey bacon, sliced tomatoes, and a spread of low-fat mayonnaise. Roll it up tightly and cut it into bite-sized pieces. This roll-up is not only delicious but also a great source of protein.

3. **Pizza Pinwheels:** Who doesn't love pizza? These pinwheels are a fun twist on the classic slice. Spread a thin layer of tomato sauce on a tortilla and sprinkle it with grated cheese. Add your favorite pizza toppings, such as sliced olives, bell peppers, and pepperoni. Roll it up tightly and cut it into bite-sized pinwheels. These pizza pinwheels are perfect for parties or as a lunchbox treat.

4. Sweet Fruit Wraps: Wraps can also be a great option for a sweet treat. Start with a tortilla and spread a layer of cream cheese or nut butter. Add sliced fruits such as strawberries, bananas, and blueberries. Drizzle with honey or sprinkle with cinnamon for an extra kick of flavor. Roll it up and enjoy a healthy and delicious dessert.

These easy-to-make wraps and roll-ups are not only tasty but also provide a balanced mix of flavors and nutrients. They are perfect for parents who want to involve their children in the kitchen and teach them about healthy meal preparation. Get creative, experiment with different fillings, and let your imagination run wild. Your kids will love these fun and tasty creations!

Fun and Healthy Snack Ideas

Snacking can be a challenging task for parents who are constantly striving to provide their children with nutritious options. However, healthy snacking doesn't have to be boring or tasteless. In fact, it can be quite fun and exciting! In this subchapter, we will explore some delicious and nutritious snack ideas that both parents and children can enjoy.

1. Fruit Kabobs: Encourage your little ones to get creative by making fruit kabobs. Simply chop up their favorite fruits such as strawberries, grapes, and pineapple, and let them skewer them onto colorful toothpicks. This snack is not only visually appealing but also packed with vitamins and antioxidants.

2. Veggie Hummus Cups: Instead of serving plain old carrot sticks, why not create veggie hummus cups? Fill small cups with hummus and stick carrot sticks, cucumber slices, and bell pepper strips into the hummus. Children will love the interactive aspect of dipping their veggies into the creamy hummus.

3. Mini Pizzas: Make snack time an interactive cooking experience by creating mini pizzas. Provide whole wheat English muffins or pita bread, and let your children top them with their favorite ingredients such as tomato sauce, low-fat cheese, and colorful veggies. Pop them in the oven for a few minutes until the cheese is melted, and voila – a delicious and healthy snack!

4. Frozen Yogurt Bites: For a cool and refreshing treat, try making frozen yogurt bites. Simply spoon flavored yogurt into small silicone molds, add a few berries or chopped fruit, and freeze until solid. These bite-sized snacks are not only fun to eat but also a great source of calcium and probiotics.

5. Ants on a Log: An all-time favorite, ants on a log is a classic snack that children adore. Spread peanut butter or cream cheese onto celery sticks and top them with raisins or dried cranberries. This snack provides a good balance of protein, healthy fats, and fiber. Remember, healthy snacking is all about balance and variety. Encourage your children to try new flavors and experiment with different ingredients. By involving them in the snack preparation process, you can instill a love for healthy eating and help them develop essential cooking skills. So, let's get creative and enjoy these fun and nutritious snack ideas together!

Chapter 5: Kid-Friendly Dinners

Homemade Pizza Night

In the chaotic world of busy schedules and demanding routines, it's crucial for families to find ways to connect and create lasting memories. And what better way to do that than by having a Homemade Pizza Night? This subchapter is dedicated to helping parents and children come together in the kitchen to prepare delicious and healthy pizzas that will tickle everyone's taste buds.

When it comes to healthy meal prep and cooking for kids, homemade pizza is an absolute winner. Not only does it allow you to control the ingredients and make healthier choices, but it also encourages children to get involved in the cooking process. Kids love to make things with their own hands, and pizza night is the perfect opportunity for them to unleash their creativity and culinary skills.

To start your Homemade Pizza Night adventure:

Gather the family around the kitchen counter and set up a pizza assembly line.

Prepare a variety of toppings like colorful veggies, lean proteins, and different types of cheese.

Encourage your children to experiment with flavors and textures, allowing them to create their own unique masterpiece.

For the health-conscious parents, choose whole wheat or whole grain crust options. These are packed with essential nutrients, fiber, and have a lower glycemic index compared to traditional pizza crusts. You can also offer gluten-free or cauliflower crusts for those with dietary restrictions.

Another tip for a healthier pizza night is to include a homemade sauce. Store-bought sauces can be high in sodium and added sugars, so why not try making your own tomato sauce using fresh tomatoes, herbs, and spices? Not only will it taste better, but it will also be a healthier alternative for your family.

Lastly, don't forget the fun factor! Turn on some lively music, put on aprons, and let the kids take charge of rolling out the dough and decorating their own pizzas. This interactive experience will boost their confidence and make them feel accomplished as they see their creations bake to perfection in the oven.

Homemade Pizza Night is not just about the end result; it's about the journey and the memories you create together. So, gather your loved ones, put on your chef hats, and embark on a delicious and healthy adventure that will bring your family closer, one slice at a time.

Build-Your-Own Tacos and Burritos

Tacos and burritos are delicious, versatile, and perfect for a fun family meal! In this subchapter, we will explore the art of building your own tacos and burritos, providing you with some healthy and tasty ideas that both parents and children will love. Get ready to unleash your creativity in the kitchen!

When it comes to building your own tacos and burritos, the possibilities are endless. Start by setting up a DIY station with all the fixings. Offer a variety of fillings such as grilled chicken, seasoned ground turkey, or black beans for a vegetarian option. Let your kids choose their favorite protein and watch their faces light up with excitement!

Next, provide an assortment of colorful vegetables to add crunch and nutrition. Sliced tomatoes, shredded lettuce, diced bell peppers, and avocado slices are all great options. Encourage your children to experiment with different combinations of toppings to create their own unique flavor profiles.

Now, let's talk about the tortillas. Offer both soft tortillas and crunchy taco shells to cater to different preferences. Whole wheat or corn tortillas are healthier choices that provide essential nutrients and fiber. Show your kids how to warm the tortillas on a skillet or in the microwave, making them more pliable and easier to fill.

To add a burst of flavor, set out an array of sauces and salsas. From mild to spicy, let your children choose their favorite condiments to personalize their tacos and burritos. Salsa verde, guacamole, and sour cream are all popular options that complement the flavors beautifully.

Building your own tacos and burritos not only encourages creativity but also promotes healthy eating. This interactive meal allows kids to take charge of their own plates, empowering them to make nutritious choices. As parents, you can rest easy knowing that your children are getting a balanced meal filled with protein, vegetables, and whole grains.

So, gather your family around the kitchen table and embark on a flavorful journey of creating your own tacos and burritos. Whether you're cooking for picky eaters or looking to introduce new flavors, this build-your-own concept will surely be a hit. Get ready to make memories and enjoy delicious, healthy meals together!

One-Pot Wonder Meals

Parents often find themselves juggling multiple responsibilities, leaving them with limited time to prepare nutritious meals for their children. However, there is a solution that can save time and still provide delicious, healthy meals for the whole family: one-pot wonder meals. These meals are not only easy to make but also require minimal cleanup, making them the perfect option for busy parents and their little ones. **One-pot wonder meals** are versatile and can be customized to suit your family's taste preferences and dietary needs. Whether your child is a picky eater or has specific dietary restrictions, these recipes offer a wide range of options to ensure everyone is satisfied at the dinner table. From vegetarian pasta dishes to hearty stews and soups, there is something for even the fussiest eaters.

The beauty of one-pot wonder meals lies in their simplicity. With just one pot, you can create a complete, balanced meal that incorporates all the necessary food groups. By combining **proteins, carbohydrates, and vegetables** in a single pot, you can save time on cooking and cleanup while still providing a nutritious meal for your family.

Not only are one-pot wonder meals convenient, but they can also be a fun way to get your children involved in the kitchen. Cooking together can be an exciting bonding activity and an opportunity to teach your kids about the importance of healthy eating. Let them help you chop vegetables, measure ingredients, or stir the pot. Not only will they feel a sense of accomplishment, but they will also be more likely to try new foods when they have a hand in preparing them.

To make the most of your one-pot wonder meals, it's essential to plan ahead. Take some time each week to create a meal plan and grocery list. This will ensure you have all the necessary ingredients on hand, making meal preparation a breeze. You can even involve your children in the planning process by asking them for their input on what meals they would like to have during the week.

In the upcoming chapters, we will provide you with a wide range of one-pot wonder meal recipes that are not only healthy but also kid-approved. From cheesy macaroni and vegetable stir-fries to flavorful chili and chicken noodle soup, these recipes will make mealtime a breeze for parents and a delight for children. So put on your aprons and get ready to embark on a culinary adventure with your little ones!

Chapter 6: Sweet Treats and Snacks

Healthy Baking with Kids

Introduction:

Baking with kids can be a fun and educational activity that not only brings families together but also encourages healthy eating habits from a young age. In this subchapter, we will explore the joys of healthy baking with your little ones. From nutritious ingredients to creative recipes, we'll provide you with all the tools you need to make baking a delightful and health-conscious experience for the whole family.

1. The Benefits of Healthy Baking with Kids:

Baking with kids offers a multitude of benefits. It fosters creativity, enhances motor skills, and teaches children about nutrition and healthy eating. By involving your little ones in the kitchen, you can instill a love for cooking and empower them to make better food choices.

2. Selecting Nutritious Ingredients:
When baking with kids, it's important to choose wholesome ingredients that are both delicious and nutritious. We'll discuss the importance of whole grains, natural sweeteners, and incorporating fruits and vegetables into your baked goods. Together, we can create tasty treats that are also good for the body.

3. Fun and Healthy Baking Recipes:
Discover a collection of delightful baking recipes that are not only enjoyable for kids but also packed with nutrients. From whole wheat banana bread to vegetable-packed muffins, each recipe is designed to satisfy young taste buds while providing essential vitamins and minerals. We'll also include gluten-free and dairy-free options for those with dietary restrictions.

4. Baking Safety Tips for Kids:
Safety is paramount when baking with children. We'll provide you with essential safety guidelines to ensure a worry-free baking experience. From handling kitchen tools to oven safety, you'll learn how to create a safe environment for your little ones.

5. Tips for Making Baking Fun:
Baking should be an enjoyable and memorable experience for both parents and children. We'll share tips on how to make baking sessions more enjoyable, including engaging your kids in age-appropriate tasks, creating themed baking sessions, and fostering a positive and encouraging environment.

Delectable Fruit-Based Desserts

Introduction:
In this subchapter, we will explore the world of delectable fruit-based desserts that are not only delicious but also healthy for both parents and children. These recipes are perfect for parents who want to introduce their children to the joys of cooking and healthy eating. Get ready to embark on a sweet and fruity adventure!

1. Berrylicious Parfait:
This simple and delightful dessert is a perfect way to incorporate fresh berries into your child's diet. Layer Greek yogurt, sliced strawberries, blueberries, and a sprinkle of granola in a glass or jar. Let your child get creative with the layers, and voila! A colorful and nutritious treat is ready to be enjoyed.

2. Tropical Fruit Popsicles:
Beat the heat with these refreshing homemade popsicles. Blend together ripe mangoes, pineapples, and bananas with a splash of coconut water. Pour the mixture into popsicle molds and freeze. These tropical fruit popsicles are a fantastic way to sneak in some extra vitamins and minerals while satisfying your child's sweet tooth.

3. Apple Nachos:

Transform a humble apple into a fun and exciting dessert by creating apple nachos. Slice apples into thin rounds and arrange them on a plate. Drizzle with melted dark chocolate and sprinkle with chopped nuts, shredded coconut, and raisins. These apple nachos are not only visually appealing but also packed with essential nutrients.

4. Watermelon Pizza:

Who says pizza has to be savory? Slice a watermelon into round discs and use them as a base for your child's creativity. Let them top the "pizza" with various fruits like sliced kiwi, strawberries, and grapes. Drizzle with honey or a yogurt sauce for an extra touch of sweetness.

5. Fruit Skewers:

Engage your child's imagination by creating fruit skewers. Thread chunks of different fruits onto bamboo skewers, such as grapes, melon balls, pineapple, and kiwi. These colorful fruit skewers are not only visually appealing but also a great way to introduce new fruits to your child's diet.

Conclusion:
These delectable fruit-based desserts are not only tasty but also provide a healthy alternative to traditional sugary treats. By involving your children in the kitchen, you can foster a love for cooking and healthy eating at an early age. So, gather your ingredients, put on your chef hats, and let the fruity adventures begin!

Guilt-Free Snack Options

Finding healthy and delicious snacks can be a challenge, especially when it comes to pleasing both parents and children. However, worry no more, as we have compiled a list of guilt-free snack options that will satisfy even the pickiest eaters. These snacks are not only tasty but also packed with essential nutrients, making them perfect for parents who prioritize healthy meal prep and cooking for kids.

1. Veggie Sticks with Hummus: Swap out those greasy potato chips for colorful veggie sticks such as carrots, cucumbers, and bell peppers. Paired with a creamy hummus dip, this snack provides a satisfying crunch while delivering a dose of vitamins and fiber.

2. Fruit Kabobs: Get creative with your fruit selection and assemble colorful fruit kabobs. From juicy pineapple chunks to succulent berries and melons, the possibilities are endless. Kids will love the vibrant presentation, and parents can rest easy knowing that their children are getting a natural sugar fix along with a variety of vitamins.

3. Yogurt Parfait: Layer low-fat yogurt with fresh fruits and granola for a delicious and nutritious snack. The yogurt provides protein and probiotics, while the fruits add natural sweetness and fiber. Top it off with a sprinkle of granola for an extra crunch.

4. Baked Sweet Potato Fries: Instead of reaching for greasy french fries, try baking sweet potato fries. Slice sweet potatoes into thin strips, toss them in a little olive oil, and bake until crispy. These fries are a fantastic source of vitamins A and C, and kids will love their sweet and savory flavor.

5. Energy Bites: Whip up a batch of energy bites using oats, nut butter, honey, and add-ins like chocolate chips or dried fruits. These bite-sized treats are perfect for on-the-go snacking, and they provide a boost of energy without the guilt of processed sugars.

6. Frozen Yogurt Popsicles: Blend together your favorite fruits and Greek yogurt, pour the mixture into popsicle molds, and freeze for a refreshing and guilt-free treat. These popsicles are a great alternative to ice cream, as they contain less sugar and provide a good source of calcium.

By incorporating these guilt-free snack options into your daily routine, you can ensure that both parents and children are nourished with wholesome ingredients. These snacks are not only delicious but also fun to make, turning healthy eating into an enjoyable experience for the whole family. So, go ahead and get creative in the kitchen, knowing that you are providing your loved ones with snacks that are both tasty and nutritious.

Chapter 7: Exploring International Cuisines

Introduction to Different Cultures' Foods

In today's diverse and interconnected world, it is essential to expose children to various cultures and their unique cuisines. Food not only nourishes our bodies but also serves as a window into different traditions, history, and lifestyles. In this subchapter, "Introduction to Different Cultures' Foods," we will embark on a culinary journey around the globe, discovering the vibrant flavors and healthy ingredients that each culture has to offer.

Exploring different cultures' foods is a fantastic way to introduce children to new tastes, textures, and aromas. It encourages them to step out of their comfort zones and appreciate the rich diversity our world has to offer. By broadening their culinary horizons, children also develop a deeper understanding and respect for people from various backgrounds.

In this chapter, we will delve into some of the most fascinating cuisines from around the world. From **the savory and aromatic spices of Indian cuisine to the fresh and vibrant flavors of Mediterranean dishes**, your taste buds are in for a treat! We will also explore the delicate balance of flavors found in **Japanese cuisine,** the bold and zesty flavors of **Mexican food**, and the comforting and hearty dishes of **Italian cooking.**

Each section will provide a brief introduction to the culture's history, traditions, and the importance of food in their daily lives. We will discuss key ingredients, cooking techniques, and even share some traditional recipes that have been adapted to suit the tastes of both parents and children.

By incorporating different cultures' foods into your family's mealtime routine, you are not only expanding your children's palates but also promoting healthier eating habits. Many traditional recipes use fresh, whole ingredients and emphasize the importance of balance and moderation.

So, whether you are looking to embark on a culinary adventure or simply add some zest to your family's meals, "Introduction to Different Cultures' Foods" will be your guide. Together, we will explore the world through its diverse and delicious cuisines, fostering a sense of appreciation for different cultures and encouraging a lifelong love for healthy and flavorful meals. Get ready to embark on a food journey that will tantalize your taste buds and nurture your curiosity!

Cooking Easy and Tasty Ethnic Dishes

In today's multicultural world, it's important for children to be exposed to a variety of flavors and cuisines. Not only does it expand their plate, but it also encourages them to embrace diversity and appreciate different cultures. That's why we've dedicated this subchapter to cooking easy and tasty ethnic dishes that both parents and children can enjoy together.

Healthy meal prep and cooking for kids can sometimes be a challenge, but with these delicious recipes, you'll find that it can be both fun and educational. By involving your children in the kitchen, you're not only teaching them valuable cooking skills, but also encouraging them to make healthier choices.

One of the simplest and most flavorful ethnic dishes you can prepare is **vegetable stir-fry with soy sauce.** This Chinese-inspired dish is packed with colorful vegetables like bell peppers, carrots, and broccoli, and is seasoned with a savory soy sauce glaze. It's a great way to introduce your children to new vegetables and show them that healthy food can be delicious too.

If you're looking to explore **Mexican cuisine**, why not try making **homemade tacos**? You can let your children help assemble the tacos by choosing their favorite fillings, such as seasoned ground turkey, shredded lettuce, diced tomatoes, and grated cheese. Not only will they enjoy the hands-on experience, but they'll also have fun customizing their tacos to their liking.

For those who want to venture into **Indian cuisine**, a flavorful and aromatic dish like **chicken curry** is a great option. You can use mild spices and adjust the heat level according to your children's taste preferences. Serve it with fluffy basmati rice and naan bread for a complete meal that will transport your taste buds to India.

Lastly, let's not forget about **Italian cuisine**. Making **homemade pizza** together can be a fun and interactive activity for the whole family. Let your children choose their favorite toppings, whether it's classic pepperoni or a combination of colorful vegetables. They'll love watching their creations come to life in the oven.

By cooking easy and tasty ethnic dishes, you're not only broadening your children's culinary horizons but also creating lasting memories in the kitchen. So, grab your aprons and get ready to embark on a culinary adventure together!

Creating a Global Food Experience at Home

In today's globalized world, exposing children to different cultures and cuisines is more important than ever. By creating a global food experience at home, parents can not only expand their children's palates but also foster an appreciation for diverse cultures. This subchapter will provide some ideas and tips on how to bring the world's flavors into your kitchen, making mealtime an exciting and educational adventure for both parents and children.

One of the best ways to create a global food experience at home is by **exploring different cuisines**. Introduce your children to the vibrant flavors of Mexican tacos, Italian pastas, Indian curries, or Japanese sushi. Encourage them to learn about the ingredients, cooking techniques, and cultural significance behind each dish. You can even turn it into a fun learning activity by researching the country's traditions and customs together.

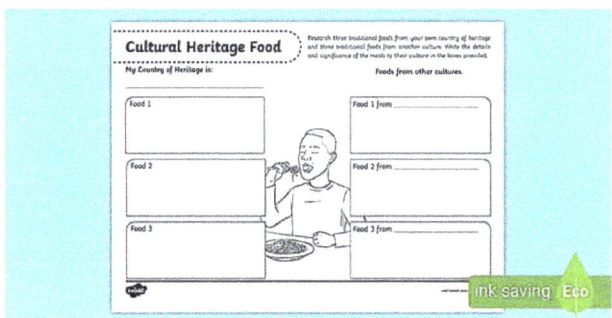

Healthy meal prep plays a vital role in creating a global food experience. By using fresh, locally sourced ingredients, parents can ensure their children are getting a nutritious and well-balanced diet. Involve your kids in the meal planning and preparation process. Let them choose a country or a specific dish they want to explore and work together to find healthy recipes that align with their preferences. This not only empowers children to make healthy choices but also instills a sense of responsibility and ownership in their mealtime routine. Cooking for kids can sometimes be a challenge, as they often have different taste preferences and can be picky eaters. However, by incorporating flavors from around the world, parents can introduce new tastes and textures in a fun and approachable way. For example, you can make **veggie-packed spring rolls** with a **sweet and tangy dipping sauce**, or create a **colorful and nutritious Buddha bowl** with a variety of toppings inspired by different cuisines. Additionally, parents can host themed dinners or cooking nights, where each family member prepares a dish from a specific country. This not only encourages creativity and teamwork but also creates an opportunity for children to showcase their culinary skills. It's a fantastic way to bond as a family and create lasting memories centered around food and culture.

In conclusion, creating a global food experience at home is a wonderful way to introduce children to different cultures, expand their palates, and promote healthy eating habits. By exploring various cuisines, involving children in meal prep, and hosting themed dinners, parents can make mealtime an enjoyable and educational adventure for the whole family. So, put on your aprons, grab your passports, and let's embark on a culinary journey together!

Chapter 8: Fun Cooking Activities and Projects

Edible Crafts for Kids

In the wonderful world of cooking, there is a special place for creativity and fun. And what better way to combine these elements than through edible crafts for kids? These delightful activities not only keep little ones entertained, but also introduce them to the joy of cooking and healthy meal prep. In this subchapter, we will explore some exciting and easy-to-make edible crafts that parents and children can enjoy together.

1. Fruit Kabobs: Encourage your little ones to create their own fruity masterpiece by threading colorful chunks of their favorite fruits onto skewers. Not only will this activity enhance their fine motor skills, but it will also introduce them to various fruits and their benefits. Let them experiment with different combinations and shapes, and watch their faces light up with pride when they take a bite of their creation.

2. Veggie Pizzas: Who says pizza can't be healthy? Provide your kids with a selection of colorful veggies, whole wheat pita bread, and a variety of low-fat cheeses. Let them design their own personal pizzas, using the veggies as toppings. This crafty activity will not only teach them about portion control but also instill a love for vegetables.

3. Rainbow Smoothies: Introduce your children to the world of smoothies by creating a rainbow-themed treat. Provide them with a range of colorful fruits, such as strawberries, bananas, blueberries, and kiwis. Let them blend these vibrant fruits with yogurt and a splash of milk to create a visually appealing and nutritious smoothie. Not only will they learn about different fruits, but they will also develop a taste for healthy snacks.

4. Ants on a Log: This classic edible craft never fails to bring a smile to children's faces. Simply provide them with celery sticks, peanut butter, and raisins. Let them spread the peanut butter onto the celery and decorate it with raisins, resembling a trail of ants. This simple yet enjoyable activity will teach them about portion control and the importance of a balanced diet.

These edible crafts are just a taste of the endless possibilities that await parents and children in the kitchen. By engaging in these activities, children will not only develop their culinary skills but also gain a deeper understanding of the importance of healthy meal prep. So, put on your aprons, gather your little ones, and embark on a delicious adventure together!

Growing Your Own Kitchen Garden

One of the most rewarding and educational activities you can do as a family is growing your own kitchen garden. Not only does it provide fresh and nutritious ingredients for your meals, but it also teaches children valuable lessons about where their food comes from and the importance of sustainable living. In this subchapter, we will explore the benefits of having a kitchen garden, tips for getting started, and some easy-to-grow vegetables and herbs that your children will love.

Benefits of Having a Kitchen Garden:

1. Fresh and Nutritious Ingredients: When you grow your own fruits, vegetables, and herbs, you have access to the freshest and most flavorful produce. This means healthier meals for your family.

2. Educational Experience: Gardening is a fun way for children to learn about nature, science, and the environment. They will gain a sense of responsibility and develop an appreciation for nature's cycles.

3. Cost-effective: Growing your own food can save you money in the long run. Plus, it reduces the carbon footprint associated with transporting produce to the grocery store.

Getting Started:

1. Choose the Right Location: Find a sunny spot in your backyard or consider using containers if you have limited space.

2. Prepare the Soil: Ensure your soil is fertile and well-draining. Add compost or organic matter to enrich it.

3. Select Easy-to-Grow Plants: Some vegetables and herbs are more forgiving for beginners. Start with tomatoes, lettuce, carrots, basil, and mint. They are hardy and quick to grow.

Easy-to-Grow Vegetables and Herbs:

1. Tomatoes: Children love picking juicy, red tomatoes straight from the vine. Cherry tomatoes are especially popular.

2. Lettuce: Grow different varieties of lettuce for colorful salads. Kids will enjoy watching the leaves grow and harvesting them.

3. Carrots: These root vegetables are fun to dig up. Choose small varieties that are perfect for snacking.

4. Basil: Plant basil for its wonderful aroma and versatility in recipes. Make homemade pesto or add fresh leaves to pizzas and pasta.

5. Mint: Mint is a fragrant herb that can be used in refreshing drinks, desserts, and even savory dishes like salads.

By growing your own kitchen garden, you can enhance your family's healthy meal prep and cooking for kids. Involve your children in every step of the process, from preparing the soil to harvesting the produce. They will develop a love for fresh food and gain essential life skills that will stay with them for years to come.

Hosting a Kids' Cooking Party

Are you looking for a fun and unique way to engage your children in the kitchen? Hosting a kids' cooking party is a fantastic opportunity to not only teach your little ones valuable cooking skills but also to create lasting memories. In this subchapter, we will guide you through the steps of hosting a successful and enjoyable kids' cooking party.

First and foremost, ensure that the recipes you choose are both delicious and healthy. Our book, "Kid-Friendly Kitchen: Fun and Healthy Recipes for Parents and Children," offers a wide variety of nutritious dishes that are sure to please even the pickiest eaters. From colorful fruit skewers to homemade veggie pizzas, our recipes are designed to make cooking fun while also promoting a balanced diet.

Next, gather all the necessary ingredients and equipment. Make a checklist and involve your children in the preparation process. This way, they will feel a sense of ownership and excitement about the upcoming party. Remember to stock up on child-sized utensils, colorful aprons, and chef hats to make the experience even more enjoyable for the kids.

Now, it's time to send out invitations to your children's friends. Let them help you design and personalize the invitations, adding an extra touch of creativity to the event. Encourage parents to RSVP with any dietary restrictions or allergies, so you can accommodate their needs and choose alternative recipes if necessary.

On the day of the party, set up a kid-friendly cooking station. Clear an area in your kitchen or dining room where the children can comfortably work. Lay out all the ingredients and utensils in an organized manner, making it easy for the kids to follow along. Divide them into small teams, assigning specific tasks to each group, such as chopping vegetables or mixing ingredients.

Throughout the party, encourage creativity and experimentation. Allow the children to add their own twists to the recipes, sparking their imaginations and fostering a sense of accomplishment. Remember, the goal is not only to create delicious food but also to instill a love for cooking and healthy eating in your children.

Finally, once the dishes are prepared, gather around the table and enjoy the fruits of your labor together. Celebrate the children's accomplishments and encourage them to share their thoughts on the experience. This will not only strengthen their bonds with each other but also create lasting memories that they will treasure for years to come.

In conclusion, hosting a kids' cooking party is an excellent way to engage your children in healthy meal prep and cooking for kids. With the right recipes, preparation, and enthusiasm, you can create a memorable experience that will inspire a lifelong love for cooking in your children. So, put on your aprons, gather your ingredients, and let the culinary adventure begin!

Chapter 9: Tips for Picky Eaters

Dealing with Selective Eating Habits

As parents, we often find ourselves frustrated and worried when our children develop selective eating habits. It can be a challenge to ensure they are getting the necessary nutrients from a well-balanced diet. However, with a little patience and creativity, we can turn mealtime into a fun and enjoyable experience for both parents and children. **One of the keys to dealing with selective eating habits** is to involve your children in the meal preparation process. By allowing them to choose ingredients, they feel a sense of ownership and are more likely to try new foods. Take them grocery shopping and let them pick out fruits, vegetables, and other healthy ingredients. This not only exposes them to a variety of foods but also helps them understand the importance of making nutritious choices.

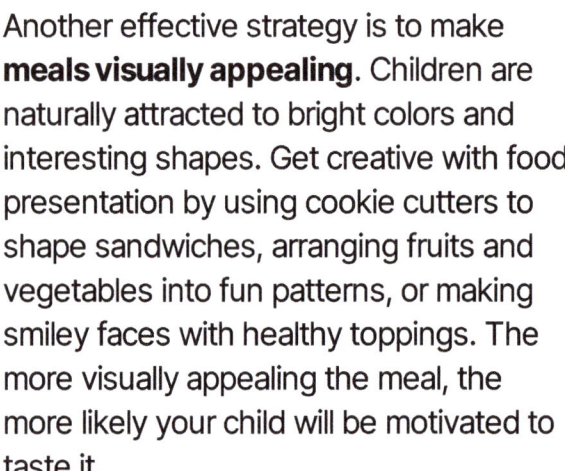

Another effective strategy is to make **meals visually appealing**. Children are naturally attracted to bright colors and interesting shapes. Get creative with food presentation by using cookie cutters to shape sandwiches, arranging fruits and vegetables into fun patterns, or making smiley faces with healthy toppings. The more visually appealing the meal, the more likely your child will be motivated to taste it.

It's also important to be patient and understanding when introducing new foods. Children's taste buds take time to develop, and it's normal for them to reject certain foods initially. Encourage your child to take small bites and praise them for trying new things, even if they don't like it. It can take several attempts before a child develops a taste for a new food, so don't give up!

Additionally, try incorporating **familiar flavors** into new dishes. If your child loves spaghetti, try adding some finely chopped vegetables into the sauce. Sneaking in vegetables this way helps expand their plate without overwhelming them. Gradually increase the quantity of vegetables over time, and before you know it, your child will be enjoying a bowl of veggie-packed spaghetti.

Remember, **creating a positive mealtime environment is crucial in dealing with selective eating habits.** Avoid pressuring or forcing your child to eat, as this can lead to negative associations with food. Instead, focus on providing a variety of healthy options and modeling good eating habits yourself.

By implementing these strategies and maintaining a patient and positive attitude, you can help your child develop a more adventurous plate and establish a healthy relationship with food. With the Kid-Friendly Kitchen, mealtime will become a joyful moment for parents and children to bond over delicious and nutritious meals.

Sneaking in Hidden Veggies

As parents, we understand the struggle of getting our children to eat their vegetables. It can be a daily battle, but fear not! We have some sneaky tricks up ourselves to help you win the war on veggies. In this subchapter, we will share some creative ways to incorporate hidden vegetables into your family's favorite meals, making mealtime healthy and fun.

One popular technique is to **puree vegetables** and mix them into dishes your kids already love. For example, you can blend some steamed carrots or spinach and add them to spaghetti sauce or meatballs. The vibrant colors and delicious flavors will go unnoticed, and your children will be getting an extra dose of nutrients without even realizing it!

Another sneaky method is to use **vegetables as a base for sauces and dips**. Instead of traditional tomato sauce, try making a sauce with roasted red bell peppers or butternut squash. These veggies add a natural sweetness and creaminess to the sauce, making it even more irresistible to little taste buds. You can also create a creamy dip with pureed cauliflower or zucchini, perfect for pairing with crunchy veggies or whole-grain crackers.

If your children are fans of baked goods, you can hide veggies in their favorite treats as well. Carrot muffins, zucchini bread, and sweet potato pancakes are all fantastic options. By using vegetables in these recipes, you not only add moisture and flavor but also boost the nutritional value of these beloved snacks.

Involving your children in the cooking process can also encourage them to try new vegetables. Let them help you wash, chop, and prepare the veggies for meals. They will feel a sense of pride in their contribution and might be more willing to taste the final product. Additionally, consider **planting a small vegetable garden** together. Watching their own plants grow and harvesting the produce can make veggies more appealing and exciting for kids.

Remember, the key is to be **creative** and **flexible**. Sneaking in hidden veggies doesn't mean you have to completely hide them. Over time, gradually increase the visibility of vegetables in your dishes, and encourage your children to explore new flavors and textures. Making mealtime an adventure can help foster a love for healthy eating in your little ones.

So, parents and children, let's embark on this exciting journey of sneaking in hidden veggies and discover a world of delicious and nutritious meals together!

Making Mealtime Fun and Stress-Free

Mealtime can often become a stressful ordeal for both parents and children. However, it doesn't have to be that way! In this subchapter, we will explore some fantastic ways to make mealtime **enjoyable, stress-free,** and even **educational.** By incorporating these ideas into your routine, you'll not only encourage healthy eating habits but also create lasting memories in the kitchen.

1. Create a Colorful Plate:
Children are naturally drawn to bright and vibrant colors. Use this to your advantage by incorporating a variety of colorful fruits and vegetables into your child's meal. Arrange them in fun shapes or patterns to make it visually appealing and exciting for them to explore.

2. Get Hands-On:
Engage your children in the meal preparation process. Let them wash the vegetables, sprinkle seasonings, or stir the batter. By involving them in the process, they will feel a sense of accomplishment and be more inclined to try new foods.

3. Story time in the Kitchen:
Make mealtime educational and entertaining by incorporating stories or fun facts about the ingredients you're using. For example, while making a tomato sauce, you can share interesting facts about tomatoes, their origins, or even tell a story about a tomato superhero.

4. Themed Meal Nights:
Designate one night a week as a themed meal night. It could be Taco Tuesday, Pizza Party Friday, or even a Breakfast-for-Dinner night. Planning themed meals adds an element of excitement and anticipation for the whole family.

5. Food Art:
Transform ordinary dishes into works of art. Encourage your children to arrange their food creatively on their plates. They can create funny faces, animals, or even landscapes using different ingredients. This not only makes mealtime fun but also encourages them to interact with their food.

6. Play Restaurant:
Transform your dining area into a restaurant by setting the table with fancy cutlery, napkins, and even a menu. Allow your children to take turns being the chef, waiter, or even the customer. This role-play activity will make mealtime feel like a special occasion.

7. Music and Dance:
Create a playlist of your children's favorite songs and play it during mealtime. Encourage them to dance or clap along, making the atmosphere lively and enjoyable. Music can help create a positive association with food and improve the overall mood at the table.

Remember, making mealtime fun and stress-free not only helps your child develop healthy eating habits but also strengthens family bonds. By incorporating these ideas into your routine, you can transform mealtime into a delightful experience for everyone involved. So, grab your aprons, put on some music, and let the fun-filled cooking adventures begin!

Chapter 10: Nurturing a Lifelong Love for Healthy Cooking

Encouraging Culinary Curiosity in Children

Introduction:
In today's fast-paced world, it can be a challenge to get children interested in healthy eating and cooking. However, instilling a love for culinary exploration in children can have numerous benefits for their overall well-being. This subchapter aims to provide parents and children with practical tips and ideas to foster culinary curiosity while making meal prep a fun and educational activity.

1. Create a Welcoming Kitchen Environment:
The first step in encouraging culinary curiosity in children is to make the kitchen an inviting space. Clear a safe area on the countertop where children can participate in meal preparation. Equip the kitchen with child-friendly utensils, colorful aprons, and chef hats to make them feel like mini-chefs.

2. Involve Children in Meal Planning:
Engage children in the meal planning process by allowing them to choose ingredients or recipes they want to try. This not only gives them a sense of ownership but also expands their culinary horizons. Encourage them to pick healthy options while guiding them to make balanced choices.

3. Make Cooking an Educational Experience:
Transform cooking into a learning opportunity by discussing the nutritional benefits of different ingredients. Teach children about portion sizes, food groups, and how various foods contribute to their health. Incorporate fun facts about fruits, vegetables, and proteins to make the experience engaging and informative.

4. Experiment with New Flavors and Textures:
Encourage children to broaden their palates by experimenting with new flavors and textures. Introduce them to different herbs, spices, and seasonings, explaining how they enhance the taste of dishes. Encourage them to try a bite of new foods even if they are initially hesitant, promoting an open-minded approach to eating.

5. Incorporate Games and Challenges:
Transform meal prep into an exciting challenge by introducing cooking games. Create a "mystery basket" challenge where children have to create a dish using specific ingredients. You can also organize cooking competitions among family members, promoting healthy competition and creativity.

6. Celebrate Achievements:
Acknowledge and celebrate children's culinary achievements, no matter how small. Display their artwork or recipes on a kitchen bulletin board to show appreciation for their efforts. This positive reinforcement will boost their confidence and inspire them to continue exploring the world of cooking.

Conclusion:
Encouraging culinary curiosity in children is a valuable investment in their long-term health and well-being. By involving children in meal planning, providing a welcoming kitchen environment, and incorporating educational experiences, parents can instill a love for cooking and healthy eating. Remember, making cooking fun and engaging will transform it into a lifelong passion for children, fostering a healthy relationship with food.

Teaching Kitchen Safety and Basic Cooking Skills

One of the most important things parents can do for their children is to teach them how to safely navigate the kitchen and develop basic cooking skills. Not only will this enable them to prepare their own meals as they grow older, but it will also instill a sense of independence and promote a healthy lifestyle. In this subchapter, we will explore essential kitchen safety tips and introduce some basic cooking skills that parents can teach their children.

Kitchen Safety Tips:

1. Always wash your hands before and after handling food.
2. Use caution when handling sharp objects like knives and scissors. Children should use kid-friendly utensils and be supervised by an adult.
3. Keep pot handles turned inward on the stovetop to prevent accidental spills.
4. Use oven mitts or pot holders to handle hot pots, pans, and baking trays.
5. Never leave the kitchen unattended while cooking.
6. Use caution when working with heat sources such as stovetops, ovens, and open flames.
7. Clean up spills immediately to prevent accidents from slips and falls.
8. Keep all electrical cords and appliances away from water sources.
9. Store cleaning supplies and chemicals in a safe place, out of reach of children.
10. Always follow recipe instructions and measurements carefully.

Basic Cooking Skills:

1. Knife Skills: Teach children how to hold and use a knife properly. Start with simple tasks like slicing soft fruits and vegetables, and gradually progress to more challenging tasks.
2. Measuring: Teach children the importance of accurate measurements in cooking. Show them how to use measuring cups and spoons correctly.
3. Mixing and Stirring: Demonstrate how to mix ingredients together using a spoon or spatula. Encourage children to use gentle, circular motions to prevent splatters.
4. Stovetop Cooking: Introduce children to stovetop cooking by starting with simple recipes like scrambled eggs or pancakes. Teach them how to adjust the heat and use pot handles safely.
5. Baking: Show children how to follow a recipe for baking cookies, cupcakes, or bread. Explain the importance of preheating the oven and using oven mitts when handling hot trays.

By teaching children kitchen safety and basic cooking skills, parents can empower them to make healthy meal choices and develop a lifelong love for cooking. Remember to always supervise children in the kitchen and make the experience fun and interactive. Cooking together can be a wonderful bonding activity that fosters creativity and promotes healthy eating habits.

Making Cooking a Family Tradition

Cooking is not just a way to prepare food; it can also be a fun and engaging activity that brings families closer together. In today's fast-paced world, where takeout and processed foods seem to dominate our meals, it is more important than ever to instill healthy cooking habits in our children. By involving them in the process, we not only teach them essential life skills but also create lasting memories and traditions.

Cooking together as a family is a fantastic way to encourage children to develop healthy eating habits. When kids are involved in meal preparation, they are more likely to try new foods and appreciate the effort that goes into making nutritious meals. It also provides an opportunity to discuss the importance of balanced nutrition and the benefits of incorporating fresh fruits, vegetables, and whole grains into our diet.

Creating a family cooking tradition can start with something as simple as planning a weekly meal together. Sit down as a family and brainstorm ideas for meals that everyone will enjoy. Encourage your children to contribute their favorite recipes or suggest new ingredients they would like to try. This not only gives them a sense of ownership but also fosters their creativity and ability to make informed choices when it comes to food.

Once you have decided on a menu, involve your children in every step of the cooking process. Assign age-appropriate tasks such as washing vegetables, measuring ingredients, or stirring the pot. This will not only help them develop important motor skills but also boost their confidence and sense of responsibility.

Make cooking a fun and interactive experience by playing music, sharing stories, or even organizing friendly cooking competitions. Encourage your children to experiment with flavors and textures, allowing them to express their individuality and develop their palate.

Beyond the immediate benefits of spending quality time together and promoting healthy eating, making cooking a family tradition has long-term advantages. As your children grow older, they will carry these skills with them, making them more self-sufficient and less reliant on processed foods. It also establishes a strong foundation for a lifetime of healthy eating and fosters a love and appreciation for home-cooked meals.

In conclusion, making cooking a family tradition is a wonderful way to bond with your children, teach them essential life skills, and promote healthy eating habits. By involving them in the meal planning and preparation process, you are not only creating lasting memories but also setting them up for a lifetime of good health and well-being. So, gather your aprons, turn on the stove, and let the family cooking traditions begin!

Chapter 11: Conclusion

Reflecting on the Journey of Cooking with Kids

Cooking with kids is not just about preparing meals. It is an incredible journey that allows parents and children to bond, create lasting memories, and instill healthy habits. In this subchapter, we will take a moment to reflect on the joys and benefits of cooking with kids, emphasizing the importance of healthy meal prep and making cooking fun for children.

Preparing nutritious meals for our children is vital for their growth and development. By involving them in the cooking process, we can teach them about the importance of making healthy food choices. Cooking together provides an opportunity to introduce various fruits, vegetables, and whole grains, allowing children to explore new flavors and textures. It also serves as an excellent platform to educate them about the benefits of balanced meals and how they impact their overall well-being.

Beyond nutritional benefits, cooking with kids offers a chance for parents and children to connect on a deeper level. The kitchen becomes a space for open communication, where parents can listen to their children's thoughts, ideas, and concerns. As children actively participate in meal preparation, they feel a sense of accomplishment, boosting their self-esteem and confidence. The shared experience of cooking creates memories that will be treasured for a lifetime.

To make cooking enjoyable for children, it is crucial to involve them in age-appropriate tasks. Younger children can wash vegetables, stir ingredients, or set the table, while older children can help with chopping, measuring, and even planning meals. Encouraging creativity and allowing children to contribute their ideas can make the experience even more exciting for them.

Furthermore, cooking with kids can be a great way to develop essential life skills. Children learn about kitchen safety, such as handling knives and hot surfaces responsibly. They also acquire valuable skills like following instructions, teamwork, and time management. By involving them in meal planning and grocery shopping, children learn about budgeting and making informed choices.

In conclusion, the journey of cooking with kids goes well beyond the creation of delicious meals. It is a transformative experience that nourishes both their bodies and souls. Through healthy meal prep and making cooking enjoyable, parents and children can build a stronger bond, create wonderful memories, and equip children with essential life skills. So, let's embrace this journey together and create a kitchen filled with love, laughter, and delectable meals.

Final Thoughts and Encouragement for Parents and Children

As we wrap up this journey through the Kid-Friendly Kitchen, we want to leave you with some final thoughts and encouragement for both parents and children. Healthy meal prep and cooking for kids can sometimes feel like a daunting task, but with the right mindset and a little creativity, it can be a fun and rewarding experience for everyone involved.

Parents, remember that you are the role models for your children when it comes to food choices and healthy eating habits. By involving them in the kitchen, you are not only teaching them valuable life skills but also fostering a positive relationship with food. Encourage their curiosity and creativity by allowing them to choose ingredients, mix flavors, and experiment with different cooking techniques. Seeing their dishes come to life will boost their confidence and make them more excited about trying new foods.

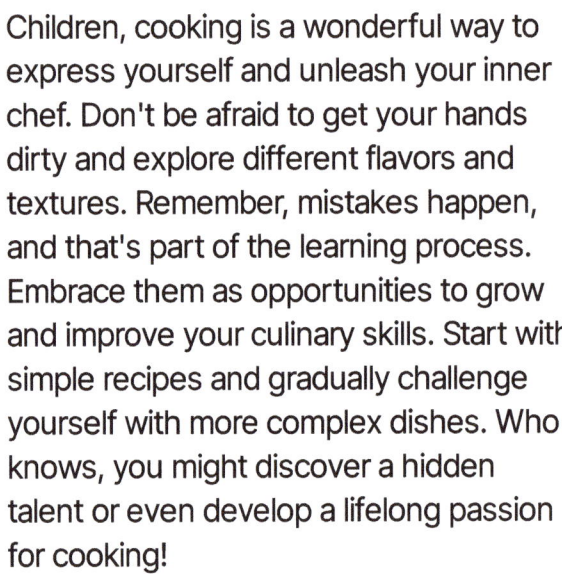

Children, cooking is a wonderful way to express yourself and unleash your inner chef. Don't be afraid to get your hands dirty and explore different flavors and textures. Remember, mistakes happen, and that's part of the learning process. Embrace them as opportunities to grow and improve your culinary skills. Start with simple recipes and gradually challenge yourself with more complex dishes. Who knows, you might discover a hidden talent or even develop a lifelong passion for cooking!

We also want to emphasize the importance of making healthy choices while still having fun. Incorporate a variety of fruits, vegetables, whole grains, and lean proteins into your meals. Experiment with different cooking methods like baking, grilling, or steaming to retain the nutritional value of your ingredients. And don't forget to balance your meals with a rainbow of colorful foods to ensure you're getting a wide range of vitamins and minerals.

Finally, remember that the kitchen is a place for bonding and creating lasting memories. Use this time to connect with your loved ones, share stories, and laugh together. Let the Kid-Friendly Kitchen be a space where you can nourish not only your bodies but also your relationships.

We hope this book has inspired you to embark on a journey of healthy cooking with your children. Remember, the kitchen is your playground, and the possibilities are endless. So gather your ingredients, turn up the music, and let the culinary adventures begin!

11 Appendix:

Kid-Friendly Kitchen Tools and Equipment Checklist

Welcome to the exciting world of cooking with your little ones! In this subchapter, we will provide you with a comprehensive checklist of kid-friendly kitchen tools and equipment. Equipping your kitchen with these essentials will not only make cooking with your children more enjoyable, but also help promote healthy meal prep and cooking for kids. So, let's get started!

1. Child-Sized Aprons and Oven Mitts: Encourage your children to wear their own aprons and oven mitts, making them feel like true chefs in the kitchen. These kid-sized accessories will protect them from any spills or burns while adding an element of fun to their cooking experience.

2. Plastic Measuring Cups and Spoons: Introduce your children to the world of measurements by providing them with colorful and easy-to-handle plastic measuring cups and spoons. This will help them understand the importance of precise measurements in cooking.

3. Safety Knives: Equip your little chefs with age-appropriate safety knives. These knives are specially designed to cut through fruits and vegetables without any risks of accidents. Encouraging your children to handle knives will develop their fine motor skills and boost their confidence in the kitchen.

4. Mixing Bowls and Whisks: Invest in a set of lightweight and durable mixing bowls and whisks. These tools are perfect for mixing ingredients, making sauces, and whisking batters. Let your children take the lead in these tasks as they learn about different textures and flavors.

5. Non-Slip Cutting Boards: Ensure safety in the kitchen by using non-slip cutting boards. These boards will prevent any accidental slips or falls while your children are chopping or slicing ingredients. Opt for vibrant and easy-to-clean cutting boards that will appeal to your little ones.

6. Silicone Baking Mats and Muffin Trays: Baking with your children can be a delightful experience. Invest in silicone baking mats and muffin trays to make the process mess-free and enjoyable. These mats and trays are non-stick, easy to clean, and perfect for creating delicious treats together.

7. Blender or Food Processor: Introduce your children to the wonders of blending and processing by using a kid-friendly blender or food processor. This versatile tool will help you create smoothies, sauces, and soups, allowing your children to experiment with flavors and textures.

Remember, the primary goal of this checklist is to make the kitchen a safe and engaging space for your children. By providing them with the right tools and equipment, you can foster their love for healthy meal prep and cooking. So, gather these kid-friendly kitchen essentials, roll up your sleeves, and embark on a culinary adventure with your little ones!

Sample Weekly Meal Plan

Planning and preparing meals for your family can sometimes feel like a daunting task, especially when you want to ensure that your children are eating nutritious and delicious food. That's why we have created a sample weekly meal plan to help make your life easier and your kids' meals more enjoyable. With a focus on healthy meal prep and cooking for kids, this meal plan aims to provide you with ideas and inspiration for creating wholesome and tasty dishes that the whole family will love.

Monday:
Breakfast - Whole-grain pancakes topped with fresh berries and a dollop of yogurt.
Lunch - Turkey and cheese roll-ups with carrot sticks and hummus for dipping.
Dinner - Baked chicken tenders served with sweet potato fries and a side of steamed broccoli.

Tuesday:
Breakfast - Scrambled eggs with spinach, tomatoes, and whole-wheat toast.
Lunch - Veggie-packed pasta salad with cherry tomatoes, cucumbers, and a light vinaigrette.
Dinner - Homemade pizza with a whole-wheat crust, topped with plenty of colorful veggies and a sprinkle of cheese.

Wednesday:
Breakfast - Overnight oats made with rolled oats, almond milk, and mixed berries.
Lunch - Grilled chicken wrap with lettuce, tomato, and a light ranch dressing.
Dinner - Baked salmon with a lemon herb crust, served with quinoa and roasted asparagus.

Thursday:
Breakfast - Yogurt parfait with layers of Greek yogurt, granola, and fresh fruit.
Lunch - Quesadillas filled with black beans, corn, and cheese, served with salsa and avocado slices.
Dinner - Turkey meatballs in marinara sauce, served over whole-wheat spaghetti and a side of roasted zucchini.

Friday:
Breakfast - Whole-grain toast topped with almond butter and sliced bananas.
Lunch - Chicken and vegetable stir-fry with brown rice.
Dinner - Baked tilapia with a crispy breadcrumb coating, served with roasted sweet potatoes and a side salad.

Saturday:
Breakfast - Fruit smoothie made with Greek yogurt, spinach, and mixed berries.
Lunch - Grilled cheese sandwich on whole-grain bread with a side of tomato soup.
Dinner - Beef tacos with whole-wheat tortillas, topped with lettuce, tomatoes, and a sprinkle of cheese.

Sunday:
Breakfast - Vegetable omelet with bell peppers, spinach, and a side of whole-wheat toast.
Lunch - Caprese salad with fresh mozzarella, tomatoes, and basil, drizzled with balsamic glaze.
Dinner - Baked chicken and vegetable skewers served with brown rice and steamed broccoli.

Remember to adapt this sample meal plan to suit your family's preferences and dietary needs. By incorporating a variety of nutritious ingredients and involving your children in the cooking process, you can make every meal a fun and healthy experience for the whole family. Enjoy!

Nutritional Guidelines for Children

Proper nutrition is essential for the healthy growth and development of children. As parents, it is crucial for us to provide our little ones with a balanced and nutritious diet that supports their physical and mental well-being. This subchapter aims to guide parents and children on the importance of healthy meal prep and offer some delicious and kid-friendly recipes to make cooking a fun and enjoyable experience. When it comes to nutrition, it's important to focus on providing a variety of foods from all food groups. A well-balanced diet should include fruits, vegetables, whole grains, lean proteins, and dairy products. Encourage your children to try new foods and flavors by involving them in the meal planning and preparation process. This will not only help them develop a healthy relationship with food but also enhance their culinary skills. When preparing meals, opt for fresh and unprocessed ingredients as much as possible.Limit the consumption of sugary snacks, sodas, and fast food, as these can lead to health problems such as obesity and dental issues. Instead, offer healthier alternatives like homemade fruit popsicles, whole-grain crackers with hummus, or homemade granola bars.Portion control is another important aspect to consider. Children have smaller stomachs, so it's crucial to offer appropriate serving sizes. Teach your children to listen to their bodies and eat until they are satisfied, rather than encouraging them to finish everything on their plate. In this subchapter, we have included a range of delicious and nutritious recipes that are perfect for children. From colorful vegetable stir-fries to homemade pizzas with hidden veggies, these recipes will make mealtime exciting and encourage your children to eat a variety of foods.

We have also included some tips and tricks for getting picky eaters to try new foods and make healthier choices. Remember, healthy eating habits start at home. By incorporating these nutritional guidelines into your daily routine and involving your children in the cooking process, you can create a positive and enjoyable experience that will set them up for a lifetime of healthy eating. Glossary of Cooking Terms One of the keys to becoming a confident cook is understanding the language of the kitchen. This glossary of cooking terms is designed to help parents and children navigate the world of culinary delights with ease. Whether you're an experienced home cook or just starting out, this glossary will be an invaluable resource in the kitchen.

1. Julienne: To cut vegetables or fruits into long, thin strips. This technique is often used for salads or stir-fries.

2. Blanch: To briefly cook vegetables or fruits in boiling water, then immediately transfer them to ice water to stop the cooking process. Blanching helps retain color, texture, and nutrients.

3. Simmer: To cook food gently in liquid at a temperature just below boiling point. Simmering is often used for soups, stews, and sauces.
4. Sauté: To cook food quickly in a small amount of oil or fat over high heat. This method is perfect for stir-frying vegetables or browning meat.
5. Zest: The outer colored part of citrus fruit peel, which is finely grated or peeled off and used to add flavor to dishes.
6. Fold: A gentle mixing technique that combines ingredients without deflating them. This is often used when incorporating whipped cream or beaten egg whites into a batter.
7. Marinade: A mixture of liquids, herbs, and spices used to soak meat, fish, or vegetables before cooking. It adds flavor and tenderizes the ingredients.
8. Roast: To cook food in an oven, usually at a high temperature, resulting in a deliciously browned exterior and tender interior.
9. Steam: To cook food by placing it in a steamer basket over boiling water. Steaming is a healthy cooking method that retains nutrients and natural flavors.
10. Mince: To chop food into tiny, uniform pieces. This technique is commonly used for garlic, onions, and herbs.

Understanding these cooking terms will empower parents and children to explore new recipes and experiment with different flavors. It will also help in creating healthy and delicious meals that the whole family can enjoy. So, grab your aprons, and let's embark on a culinary adventure together!

www.ingramcontent.com/pod-product-compliance
Lightning Source LLC
LaVergne TN
LVHW072128060526
838201LV00071B/4991